Photography by Jacqui Melville

Blitz

Blender recipes
without a
smoothie in sight

JULIET BAPTISTE-KELLY

Contents

Introduction

When bullet blenders first hit the shops they made nutritious smoothies available to everyone. Quickly, easily and tastily you could whip up a delicious smoothie with whatever you had at home. The recipes in *Blitz* take that same ease and speed and open your kitchen to a whole host of other recipes; pastries, ice creams, sauces, dips and cakes. There's no need to buy extra equipment, just follow the recipes and get even more out of your bullet blender. Whether you still make a smoothie each morning or your blender is gathering dust in a cupboard, here is a collection of recipes which will change the way you look at your bullet blender for good.

Before you start, it's worth noting that your bullet blender will usually have been supplied with two blades.

One has two or four prongs that point upwards; this is an **extraction blade**. It creates a centrifuge, or whirlpool effect, so works best for combining things with some liquid content as ingredients get sucked towards the blades and mixed up.

The second blade is a **milling blade**; it spins and pulverises whatever you place into the cup. You can use it to grind nuts or make breadcrumbs; it will make fantastic nut flours. Because it can only grind things that come directly into contact with the blades, it won't mix large volumes or liquids well. Luckily, your cup fits both blades so you can switch between the two for different steps of the recipes.

Unless otherwise stated all the recipes will use the extraction blade.

If using a fan oven, reduce the heat by 10–20°C (50–68°F), but check with your handbook, as all ovens vary.

Batters

Batters are so simple in a bullet blender –
putting all the ingredients into the cup to mix is a lot
less messy than using a more traditional whisk and the
results are always fluffy and light. Suddenly, making
pancakes for breakfast at home isn't such a chore!

Fluffy Breakfast Pancakes

makes 12
–

300 ml (10 fl oz) buttermilk • 30 g (1 oz) butter, melted • splash of vanilla extract
1 egg • 230 g (8 oz/generous 1¾ cups) self-raising flour
1 tablespoon sugar • 1 teaspoon baking powder

The centrepiece of a great brunch, these fluffy pancakes can be enjoyed with fruit, syrup or bacon.

method

Fill the cup of your blender with the buttermilk, butter, vanilla and egg in first, followed by the flour, sugar and baking powder. Blitz for a few seconds, shake the cup and blitz again until you have a smooth, thick batter.

Warm a non-stick frying pan (skillet) on a low to medium heat for a few minutes before starting with your first pancake. Spoon a 1.5 cm (3 in) wide dollop of batter into your hot pan and leave to cook until you see bubbles coming to the surface, then flip them over to cook the other side. Repeat until you have used up all the batter. Enjoy with syrup and blueberries.

Frozen Banana Pancakes

makes 10
–

100 g (3½ oz/1⅓ cups) plain yoghurt, plus extra to serve (optional)
200 g (7 oz/1½ cups) buckwheat flour • 1 frozen banana • 1 egg • 2 tablespoons honey
2 tablespoons cocoa powder • 1 tablespoon almond or flavoured nut oil
50 g (2 oz/1⅓ cups) chopped dates

Rather than throw out overripe bananas, peel and freeze them to use later. Frozen bananas are a useful ingredient in bullet blender recipes and here, along with dates, nutty buckwheat and cocoa, they make for a sweet, chocolatey pancake without any added sugar.

method

Fill the cup of your blender in the order opposite, leaving out the dates. Blitz for a few seconds, shake the cup and blitz again until you have a thick batter. Give the batter a stir, and add the dates. Blitz for a very few seconds to mix them up.

Warm a non-stick frying pan (skillet) over a low medium heat for a few minutes before starting with your first pancake. Spoon a 7.5 cm (3 in) wide dollop of batter into the hot pan and leave to cook until you see bubbles coming to the surface on the uncooked side, then flip the pancake over to cook the other side. Repeat until you have used up all the batter – after the first one, which allows you to gauge cooking time and temperature of the pan, you should be able to cook several at once. Enjoy them hot with yoghurt and date syrup or fresh fruit, or leave them to cool and eat them like drop scones.

Crêpes

makes 10

—

125 g (4 oz/1 cup) plain (all-purpose) flour • 1 egg
285 ml (10 fl oz) whole milk • pinch of salt
splash of vegetable oil

A classic and simple recipe for when Pancake Day comes around. Using your bullet blender to mix the batter brings a smoothness and airiness to thin pancakes, and pouring straight from the cup makes cooking crêpes even less messy.

method

Put everything, apart from the oil, into the cup of your blender and blitz to a smooth, creamy batter. Leave to rest for 30 minutes.

Heat a non-stick frying pan (skillet) over a medium–high heat for a few minutes before adding the oil. Give the batter a final quick blitz then pour in enough to coat the bottom of the pan, tilting it to let the batter swirl around and create a thin, even layer over the base. Shuffle the frying pan, to see if the pancake is cooked enough to come away from the base; if it is, you can turn (or flip) to finish off the other side. Try piling your crêpes with homemade Chocolate Spread (page 110) and cream.

Pikelets

makes 12

—

150 ml (5 fl oz) lukewarm water • ½ of 7 g (1¼ oz) sachet easy yeast
75 ml (2½ fl oz) whole milk • 1 tablespoon honey
160 g (5½ oz/1⅓ cups) self-raising flour • ½ teaspoon salt
½ teaspoon bicarbonate of soda (baking soda)

Just the thing for chilly mornings or teatimes – and not to be confused with Antipodean pikelets – these mini crumpets originate from the Midlands, are quick to make and require very little time to prove before their bubbly batter can be cooked in a hot pan and served with butter and jam.

method

Mix the lukewarm water with the yeast in a jug to encourage it to dissolve, then stir in the milk and honey. Measure the flour into the cup of your blender and pour on the liquid. Screw the lid on securely and blitz for 30 seconds until smooth. Leave the batter to rest (with the lid removed) for 30 minutes.

Sprinkle over the salt and bicarbonate of soda, stir and leave for a further 15 minutes.

Heat a non-stick frying pan (skillet) over a medium heat for a few minutes to get evenly warm and spoon a 7.5 cm (3 in) puddle of batter into the pan. Wait for bubbles to start popping and setting before turning over to cook the other side.

As with crumpets, these are best crisped up in a toaster or under a grill (broiler), so leave to cool for at least 5 minutes before toasting.

Courgette Fritters

makes 8

—

150 ml (5 fl oz) buttermilk • 180 g (6 oz/1½ cups) self-raising flour
½ teaspoon paprika • 1 large courgette (zucchini), grated
1 egg • 1 teaspoon baking powder • ½ teaspoon bicarbonate of soda (baking soda)
pinch of salt • ¼ teaspoon ground black pepper • vegetable oil for frying

Thick, tasty and easy; these are fabulous topped with a poached egg, fresh herbs and some chilli flakes.

method

Fill the cup of your blender in the order opposite, leaving out roughly half the courgette and not including the oil. Blitz for 10 seconds or so, shake the cup and blitz again, repeating until you have a thick batter. Add the rest of the courgette and stir.

Warm a non-stick frying pan (skillet) over a medium heat for a few minutes, add a little oil and swirl it around the pan before starting with your first fritter. Dollop a 10 cm (4 in) mound of batter into the pan and leave to cook until the base has browned to a golden crust, around 2 minutes, then flip the fritter over and cook the other side. Repeat until you have used up all of the batter, adding more oil as necessary.

Cornbread

makes 1 small pan

–

200 ml (7 fl oz) buttermilk • 150 g (5 oz/1 cup) fine cornmeal (or polenta if you can't
get hold of cornmeal) • 100 g (3½ oz) butter, softened, plus 40 g (1½ oz) for cooking
3 teaspoons caster (superfine) sugar • 50 g (2 oz/1⅓ cups) frozen sweetcorn
½ teaspoon salt • 1 teaspoon baking powder
½ teaspoon bicarbonate of soda (baking soda) • ½ teaspoon chipotle chilli flakes

20

An American favourite, try it with chilli con carne or vegetable stews instead of rice or potatoes.

method

Preheat the oven to 230°C (450°F/Gas 8). Put the ingredients into the cup of your blender in the order opposite (except for the butter for cooking), put the lid on and give it a shake. Blitz for 20 seconds, shake or stir the contents and blitz again until you have a smooth, fairly liquid batter.

Melt the remaining butter in a small ovenproof frying pan (skillet) until it starts to foam. Pour the batter into the melted butter – it should fill the pan to just below the rim. Put the pan into the hot oven and cook for 25–30 minutes, until cooked through and golden brown on top. Once it's done, remove the cornbread from the oven and leave to cool for 5 minutes before lifting out of the pan and enjoying dunked into a chilli or served with guacamole and eggs.

Cakes & Puddings

Seeing my friend make a brownie in a bullet blender a few years ago was a revelation! The size of the cup makes for an ideal amount of mix in a standard cake tin, and the all-in nature of mixing up cakes in your blender means you can't go wrong, even if baking isn't your strong point.

Orange &
Almond Cake

makes 1 medium cake

–

1 large orange • 2 eggs
150 g (5 oz/1½ cups) ground almonds (almond meal) • 70 g (2½ oz) lemon curd
70 g (2½ oz/⅓ cup) caster (superfine) sugar

**Moist and rich, without being too sweet, this
is a fabulous dessert cake, best enjoyed with
a spoonful of gently whipped cream on top.**

method

Begin by placing the whole orange, unpeeled,
in a pan of boiling water – make sure there's
enough water to completely cover the orange
– and simmer for at least an hour, until the
fruit is tender and cooked all the way through.
Remove from the heat, drain and leave the
orange aside until it is cool enough to handle.
Grease and flour a 20 cm (8 in) springform
cake tin, lining the bottom with baking paper.

Preheat the oven to 170°C (338°F/Gas 3).
Once the orange has cooled, cut it into eight
segments, removing any pips. Put the orange,
skin and all, into the cup of your blender
and blitz to a pulp. Add the eggs, followed
by the ground almonds, lemon curd then
the sugar and blitz again until everything
is incorporated into a smooth mixture. Pour
the batter into the prepared tin and bake
in the oven for 40 minutes. Check the cake
is cooked by inserting a skewer – if it comes
out clean the cake is done. Remove from
the oven and leave to cool in the tin.

Chocolate Melt-in-the-middle Puddings

makes 4

—

75 g (2½ oz) butter, softened • 100 g (3½ oz/½ cup) soft brown sugar
40 g (1½ oz/1⅓) cocoa powder • 150 g (5 oz/1¼ cups) self-raising flour
100 ml (3½ fl oz) whole milk • 1 egg • 4 tablespoons Chocolate Spread (page 110)

The Chocolate Spread on page 110 works very well here – perfect for that delicious oozing, melting chocolate centre.

method

Preheat the oven to 180°C (356°F/Gas 4).

Mix all the ingredients, except the chocolate spread, in the cup of your blender to form a smooth, runny cake batter.

Butter and flour four individual dariole or pudding moulds, and line the bottoms with a circle of baking paper. Put a tablespoon of pudding mixture into the base of each mould, carefully add a dollop of chocolate spread in the centre of the pudding mix and then fill the rest of the mould with pudding batter, stopping 1 cm (½ in) below the rim.

Place into the hot oven for around 15 minutes, until the cake batter on top has set (the puddings will still have some wobble thanks to the centres). Once cooked, carefully slide a knife around the edge of the puddings and turn out onto individual plates, remembering to remove the paper discs. Eat while still hot so the chocolate spread centre can ooze out onto your plate.

Courgette Loaf Cake

makes 1 medium loaf

–

*200 g (7 oz) grated courgette (zucchini) • 150 g (5 oz/⅔ cup) caster (superfine) sugar
100 ml (3½ fl oz) vegetable oil • 1 egg • 1 teaspoon vanilla extract
½ teaspoon ground nutmeg • pinch of ground cloves
¼ teaspoon baking powder • ½ teaspoon bicarbonate of soda (baking soda)
200 g (7 oz/1⅔ cups) self-raising flour*

Courgette (zucchini) coupled with nutmeg and vanilla bring a smooth, creamy flavour to this easy loaf cake, which is the perfect accompaniment to a cup of tea.

method

Preheat the oven to 180°C (356°F/Gas 4) and line medium loaf tin (30 x 12 cm/12 x 5 in) with baking paper.

Place all the ingredients, except for the flour, in the cup of your blender and blitz to a smooth liquid. Add the flour, stir, then blitz until all the flour is incorporated. Pour into your prepared loaf tin and bake for 45 minutes, until the top is golden brown and a skewer inserted into the centre of the cake comes out clean.

Ginger & Lemon Slice

makes 10
–

100 g (3½ oz/½ cup) ground almonds (almond meal) • 100 g (3½ oz) lemon curd
50 g (2 oz/¼ cup) caster (superfine) sugar, plus extra to sprinkle on top
1 egg • zest and juice of 1 lemon • ½ teaspoon baking powder
1 quantity of Ginger Crunch Cheesecake Base (page 40)

A tribute to the delicious slice available on the counters of Leon restaurants across London, this is a quick, easy and incredibly moreish cake, which keeps well for up to five days, and just happens to be gluten-free too.

method

Preheat the oven to 180°C (356°F/Gas 4), and butter and line a 20 x 20 cm (8 x 8 in) cake tin with baking paper.

Place all the ingredients into the cup of your blender, except for the ginger biscuit base, saving half the lemon juice for later. Blitz to a smooth, thick batter.

Line the base of the tin with the ginger biscuit mixture, flattening and smoothing it before pouring the lemon cake batter on top. Bake for 30 minutes, then insert a skewer into the centre of the cake to check it is cooked – it will still be a little damp but the lemon cake should have a crumb, rather than be liquid.

Once cooked, remove from oven, sprinkle with caster sugar and squeeze the remaining lemon juice on top. Leave to cool before cutting into fingers.

Banana
Malt Loaf

makes 1 medium loaf

–

150 ml (5 fl oz) boiling water • 100 g (3½ oz/generous ½ cup) sultanas • 1 teabag
1 frozen banana • 150 g (5 oz) malt extract • 150 g (5 oz/1¼ cups) plain (all-purpose) flour
70 g (2½ oz/½ cup) wholemeal flour • 2 teaspoons baking powder

This is a great breakfast loaf. Not too sweet, it toasts well and, though it's less sticky than store-bought malt loaves, it still packs a deep malty flavour.

method

Preheat the oven to 180°C (356°F/Gas 4) and line a loaf tin with baking paper.

Pour the boiling water over the sultanas and teabag and leave to steep for 20 minutes.

Once the sultanas have plumped up nicely, drain the soaking water into the cup of your blender (discarding the teabag and saving the sultanas for later) and add the banana, malt extract, flours and baking powder and blitz to a thick batter. Add the sultanas and give a stir before pouring the malt loaf mixture into the prepared loaf tin.

Bake for 1 hour until a skewer inserted into the centre of the loaf comes out clean. Leave to cool in the tin, before turning out.

Chocolate Espresso Cake

makes 1 medium cake

–

200 g (7 oz) butter • 2 tablespoons espresso or strong instant coffee
100 g (3½ oz) dark chocolate (minimum 70% cocoa), broken into pieces
200 g (7 oz/1½ cups) toasted hazelnuts • 150 g (5 oz/¾ cup) muscovado sugar
3 tablespoons cocoa powder • 2 eggs plus 2 egg yolks

A flourless cake with dark, rich flavours, which looks and tastes like it has taken a lot more effort to produce than using a blender.

method

Preheat the oven to 180°C (356°F/Gas 4). Butter and flour a 20 cm (8 in) springform cake tin, lining the base with baking paper.

Melt the butter with the espresso in a saucepan or microwave, and put the chocolate into the hot butter coffee mixture to melt for 2 minutes before stirring to a smooth paste. Leave to cool briefly.

Grind the hazelnuts to a fine powder using the flat milling blade of your blender.

Add the sugar, cocoa powder and eggs to the ground hazelnuts and change to the four-pronged extraction blade. Mix until smooth.

Once the chocolate–coffee mix has cooled enough to use (it must be below 60°C/140°F or it will scramble the eggs when you introduce it to the blender!), tip it into the cup of your blender to combine with the sugar, nuts and eggs, blitzing in short pulses.

Turn out into the prepared tin, smooth the top and bake for 50 minutes, or until the cake has set in the centre and is beginning to come away from the sides.

Traditional Cheesecake Base

makes 1 medium cheesecake base

–

60 g (2 oz) butter • 2 tablespoons golden syrup (or dark corn syrup)
200 g (7 oz) digestive biscuits (or graham crackers), broken into pieces
1 teaspoon sea salt

A good cheesecake is a thing of great joy. As well as this traditional cheesecake base, there follow recipes for two more bases and three cheesecake toppings, which you can mix and match as you see fit.

method

Melt the butter with the golden syrup (no need to boil) in a saucepan or microwave. Butter a 20 cm (8 in) round springform tin and line it with baking paper.

Put the digestives into the cup of your blender in three batches, adding the salt as you go. Using the milling blade, blitz the first batch to a chunky powder, tip out into the prepared tin and repeat the crushing with the remaining biscuits. Pour the butter and golden syrup mixture all over the crushed biscuits and spread the mixture evenly, pressing down firmly to create a smooth layer.

Put into the fridge to chill for at least an hour before you top with your chosen cheesecake.

Chocolate Cheesecake Base

makes 1 medium cheesecake base
–

150 g (5 oz) Bourbon Biscuits (page 60), roughly chopped
50 g (2 oz) Maltesers (or Whoppers) • pinch of salt
60 g (2 oz) butter, melted

This is my go-to chocolate base, and it's tempting to just eat it on its own! If you've not made the bourbon biscuits from the book, then shop bought bourbons (chocolate cream cookies) are fine.

method

Put the biscuits in the freezer for an hour or so. Butter a 20 cm (8 in) round springform tin and line it with baking paper.

Once frozen, put the biscuits into the cup of your blender with the Maltesers and salt. Blitz to a crumb using a milling blade, tip out into a bowl and add the butter and stir. Tip the sticky chocolate biscuit base mixture into the prepared tin and press down firmly – if you cover the base mixture with cling film (plastic wrap) and press down with the bottom of a glass, it avoids pulling up any sticky patches.

Put into the fridge for at least an hour to set.

Ginger Biscuit Cheesecake Base

makes 1 medium cheesecake base

–

75 g (2½ oz) frozen cubed butter, plus extra for greasing
100 g (3½ oz/⅔ cup) fine cornmeal or polenta • 10 g (½ oz) ground ginger
50 g (2 oz/¼ cup) soft brown sugar • pinch of salt
30 g (1 oz) blanched almonds, roughly chopped

I always keep a batch of cubed butter in a resealable bag in the freezer, for making pastries and biscuits in the bullet blender. The difference with using frozen butter to make dough is amazing.

method

Preheat the oven to 180°C (356°F/Gas 4). Butter a 20 cm (8 in) round springform tin and line it with baking paper.

Place everything, with the exception of the almonds, into the cup of your blender, shake to distribute and blitz to a biscuit dough consistency. Add the almonds to the dough, give a gentle stir, then blitz again (it's good to keep them a little chunky). Tip the ginger dough into the prepared tin and press down firmly to form an even layer. Bake in the oven for 20 minutes, unless you're using this base with a cheesecake top that requires baking, in which case there is no need to precook it – just layer on your topping and bake both at the same time.

Classic Vanilla Cheesecake

makes 1 medium cheesecake

–

*base of your choice (pages 36–41) • 450 g (1 lb) full-fat cream cheese
100 g (3½ oz) sour cream • 150 g (5 oz/⅔ cup) caster (superfine) sugar
1 tablespoon cornflour (cornstarch) • 1 teaspoon vanilla bean paste
2 eggs, plus 2 egg yolks*

You can't go wrong with a vanilla cheesecake, this one is easy; and letting it cool in the oven for an hour should stop the top from cracking.

method

Preheat the oven to 150°C (300°F/Gas 2).

Put everything except the egg yolks in the cup of your blender and blitz. Add the yolks and blitz again. Give the whole mixture a good shake to make sure it's smooth and pour out onto your base of choice.

Bake for 45 minutes – it should have risen a little and be slightly browned on top with a slight wobble in the centre. Leave to cool in the switched-off oven for 1 hour before allowing to cool completely at room temperature and putting in the fridge to settle.

No-bake Chocolate Cheesecake

makes 1 medium cheesecake
–
base of your choice (pages 36–41) • 200 ml (7 fl oz) double (heavy) cream
100 g (3½ oz) good-quality dark chocolate (minimum 70% cocoa), broken into pieces
50 g (2 oz/scant ½ cup) icing (confectioner's) sugar • 150 g (5 oz) full-fat cream cheese

This cheesecake is rich and delicious, definitely not one for the kids and paired with the subtle heat of the Ginger Biscuit Base (page 40) makes a fantastic dessert.

method

Bring 150 ml (5 fl oz) of the cream nearly to the boil in a saucepan or bowl if microwaving. Add the broken chocolate to the scalded cream and leave for 1 minute to melt, then stir to a smooth ganache and leave to cool.

In the cup of your blender mix the icing sugar, cream cheese and remaining cream to a smooth mixture. Add the ganache, stir briefly and replace the lid for a final blitz to mix well. Scoop the chocolate cheesecake mixture on top of your chosen base, smooth the top and put in the fridge to set for 2 hours.

Caramel Cheesecake

makes 1 medium cheesecake

–

base of your choice (pages 36–41)
59 g (2 oz) pack Angel Delight butterscotch dessert mix (butterscotch instant pudding mix)
250 g (9 oz) full-fat cream cheese • 150 ml (5 fl oz) whole milk • 50 g (2 oz) sour cream
300 g (10½ oz) canned or bottled caramel sauce

This recipe is very easy and uses a childhood favourite to create a slightly more grown-up dessert.

method

Mix the butterscotch powder, cream cheese, milk, cream and half of the caramel sauce in the cup of your blender until you have a thick, smooth mixture.

Dot your chosen base with a few spoonfuls of the remaining caramel sauce and pour half of the cheesecake mix onto the base. Add more spoonfuls of caramel, fill the tin with the rest of the cheesecake mix and use the last of the caramel to dot the top of the cheesecake. Using a spatula or spoon, make several swirls through the mix to create a caramel ripple, smooth the top and put in the fridge to chill and set for at least 2 hours.

Pastry
& Biscuits

Making pastry in a bullet blender is the perfect shortcut, so that rustling up a quick quiche for lunch or tart for dinner becomes a breeze. Making sure you've got some frozen cubed butter stashed in your freezer will mean you can knock up homemade pastry or biscuits in a matter of minutes.

Short & Sweet Pastry

makes 350 g (12 oz) pastry

–

100 g (3½ oz) frozen cubed butter • 150 g (5 oz/1¼ cups) plain (all-purpose) flour
75 g (2½ oz/scant ⅔ cup) icing (confectioner's) sugar
1 egg yolk • zest of ½ lemon • ½ teaspoon vanilla bean paste

I store around 500 g (1 lb 2 oz) of frozen cubed butter in a resealable sandwich bag in my freezer, for making pastry and biscuits. It will keep for up to six months, and it's well worth spending a few minutes chopping butter and stashing it away to make these easy pastries.

method

Place half the butter, the flour and sugar into the cup of your blender, put the lid on and shake well, then blitz to a breadcrumb consistency. Tip out into a bowl.

Put the remaining butter, the egg yolk, lemon zest and vanilla, followed by the blitzed flour mixture, into the cup of your blender, shake, then blitz to a dough.

It will be quite crumbly but tip it out onto a well-floured work surface and bring together into a soft dough with your hands. Chill, wrapped in cling film (plastic wrap), until needed.

Rough Puff Pastry

makes 500 g (17½ oz) pastry

–

200 g (7 oz/1⅔ cups) plain (all-purpose) flour, plus extra for dusting
50 g (2 oz) butter, softened • 50 ml (2 fl oz) water
½ teaspoon salt • 70 g (2½ oz) frozen cubed butter

Puff pastry is time-consuming and can be a daunting prospect. Rough puff, on the other hand, is a lot simpler. It gives a similar flaky, buttery result but with much less effort required.

However, this does take a little time, but it's mostly the resting intervals between rolling out the butter-studded pastry, and the outcome is well worth the investment.

method

Place half the flour, the softened butter, water and salt into the cup of your blender. Blitz to a sticky paste. Scrape down the sides of the cup and add the frozen butter. Blitz again for a few pulses – you will have a lumpy, gluey-looking mix. Put the remaining flour in a bowl and scrape the dough onto it, swiftly mixing to incorporate the flour. Wrap the pastry in cling film (plastic wrap) and leave to rest in the fridge for 45 minutes.

Once it has rested, place the pastry on a well-floured surface and, using a well-floured rolling pin, roll it to a rectangle approximately 25 x 15 cm (10 x 6 in), with the longer sides running vertically. Dust the surface of the pastry with flour and fold the top third over, leaving the bottom third exposed. Bring the bottom third to cover the first fold – you should be left with a thick rectangle of pastry approximately 7.5 x 15 cm (3 x 6 in). Press this down with the rolling pin to flatten it a little, wrap in cling film and return to the fridge for a further 45 minutes.

Repeat the rolling and folding as above; you will still be able to see lumps of butter and some will invariably come to the surface as you flatten and stretch the pastry. If this happens, just flour the patch well and carry on – these seams of butter will give the pastry a wonderful flaky crunch. Return the pastry to the fridge for a final 45 minutes. Give the pastry a last roll and fold, then, rather than wrapping it up, continue to roll out into a sheet of pastry ready to use.

Savoury Pie Pastry

makes 400 g (14 oz) pastry

–

100 g (3½ oz) frozen cubed butter • 250 g (9 oz/2 cups) plain (all-purpose) flour
1 teaspoon mustard powder • 1½ teaspoons salt
1 egg, beaten • 3 teaspoons cold water

This is a versatile, savoury pastry for quiches and pies. The frozen butter makes it easy to handle at the beginning and keeps the pastry rich and crumbly.

method

Place the butter, flour, mustard powder and salt in the cup of your blender, making sure you put the butter in first. Shake, then blitz for a few short bursts until the mixture resembles breadcrumbs. Tip the crumby mixture onto a clean work surface and make a well in the centre. Add the egg and water, then bring the ingredients together with your hands to make smooth pastry, wrap well in cling film (plastic wrap) and rest in the fridge for at least 30 minutes.

Fig Rolls

makes 12
–

300 g (10½ oz) dried figs, woody stems removed • 100 ml (3½ fl oz) boiling water
50 g (2 oz) date syrup • zest of ½ lemon • pinch of ground nutmeg
pinch of ground cinnamon • pinch of ground cloves
1 quantity of Short & Sweet Pastry (page 50) • a little milk to seal and glaze

Fig rolls are a cookie jar favourite of mine, making your own is very satisfying and means you can tweak the flavour to suit your palate.

method

Preheat the oven to 180°C (356°F/Gas 4) and line a baking tray with baking paper or a silicone mat.

Chop the figs and put into a bowl with the boiling water and date syrup. Leave to soak for at least 20 minutes.

Put the figs and their soaking water into the cup of your blender with the lemon zest and spices. Blitz to a thick paste. Roll out the pastry on a sheet of baking paper (stick the corners down with masking tape if it moves around a lot) to a 30 x 12.5 cm (12 x 5 in) rectangle. Spoon the fig paste into sausage shape 5 cm (2 in) wide along the long edge of the pastry, leaving a little room at the very edge to act as a seam. Wet the seam with milk and use the baking paper to lift the long side of the pastry furthest from you, up and over the fig sausage. Gently press the seam closed then wrap the fig roll sausage in paper, twisting the ends like a Christmas cracker. Roll the paper package backwards and forwards to set the seam and give you a tightly packed biscuit.

Chill in the fridge for 20 minutes, then remove the baking paper and slice the sausage into biscuits 3 cm (1 in) long. You can keep the slices circular or flatten to a more traditional roll shape. Place on the prepared baking tray, seam side down, brush with milk and bake for 25 minutes.

Moo-cow Biscuits

makes 15
—

75 g (2½ oz) butter, softened
100 g (3½ oz) malt extract (available from health food stores)
50 g (2 oz) Horlicks or Ovaltine powder (or malted milk powder) • 1 egg
pinch of salt • 275 g (10 oz/2¼ cups) plain (all-purpose) flour

A teatime classic. Malted milk biscuits – or moo-cow biscuits, as they were always known in my house – are fun and quick to make.

method

Preheat the oven to 180°C (356°F/Gas 4) and line a baking tray with baking paper or a silicone mat.

Put all the ingredients, except for the flour, into the cup of your blender and blitz to a creamy mixture. Add the flour, give a brief stir and blitz again until you have a smooth biscuit dough. Scrape out of the cup onto cling film (plastic wrap), wrap tightly and put in the fridge to chill for at least 20 minutes.

When the dough has firmed up, carefully (it is a very soft dough) roll it out onto a well-floured surface to a thickness of 1 cm (½ in) and cut into 5 x 4 cm (2 x 1½ in) rectangles, using a fork, press a pattern around the edges of the biscuits. Place on the prepared baking tray, leaving 2.5 cm (1 in) in between each biscuit. Bake for 12 minutes.

Bourbon Biscuits

makes 10
–

200 g (7 oz/1⅔ cups) plain (all-purpose) flour • 100 g (3½ oz/½ cup) soft brown sugar
75 g (2½ oz/1⅔ cups) cocoa powder • 1 teaspoon bicarbonate of soda (baking soda)
½ teaspoon salt • 125 g (4 oz) frozen cubed butter
2 tablespoons golden syrup (or dark corn syrup) • 4 tablespoons whole milk
For the buttercream filling: 50 g (2 oz) skimmed milk powder
100 g (3½ oz/generous ¾ cup) icing (confectioner's) sugar • 3 tablespoons cocoa powder
75 g (2½ oz) unsalted butter, softened • 1 teaspoon golden syrup (or dark corn syrup)
1 tablespoon whole milk • pinch of salt

A dark chocolate sandwich biscuit (cookie) perfect for dunking in a hot drink.

method

Preheat the oven to 180°C (356°F/Gas 4) and line a baking tray with baking paper or a silicone mat.

Put the flour, sugar, cocoa powder, bicarbonate of soda and salt into the cup of your blender and blitz to combine. Add the butter, shake and blitz again to distribute the butter. Finally, add the golden syrup and milk and blitz to bring the dough together. Tip the biscuit dough out onto a piece of cling film (plastic wrap) and briefly knead to make sure it is mixed well. Wrap and place in the fridge for 30 minutes to firm up.

Meanwhile, make the buttercream filling. Blitz the dry ingredients together to distribute the cocoa and milk powder, then add the butter, golden syrup and milk and blitz to a smooth icing (frosting) – you might need to scrape down the sides and blade a few times and pulse to achieve a spreadable paste.

Roll out the biscuit dough between two sheets of cling film or baking paper to a rectangle shape with a thickness of 5 mm (¼ in). Remove the top layer of cling film or paper and cut the dough into even finger shapes. Using a palette knife, lift the Bourbon fingers onto the prepared baking tray and bake for 15 minutes. Leave to cool on a wire rack. When they have hardened, spread a teaspoon of buttercream on one biscuit and place a second on top. Continue sandwiching the biscuits until you have used up all the chocolate biscuit fingers and filling.

Garibaldi Biscuits

makes 16
–

150 g (5 oz/1¼ cups) plain (all-purpose) flour
50 g (2 oz/¼ cup) caster (superfine) sugar • 50 g (2 oz) frozen cubed butter
50 ml (2 fl oz) whole milk, plus extra for glazing • 125 g (4 oz/generous ¾ cup) currants

'Squashed fly biscuits' often divide opinion in the biscuit-eating world, but I love the simplicity of the currant-studded shortbread.

method

Preheat the oven to 180°C (356°F/Gas 4) and line a baking tray with baking paper or a silicone mat.

Put the flour, sugar and butter into the cup of your blender, shake and blitz to a breadcrumb consistency. Add the milk and pulse into a dough. Tip out onto cling film (plastic wrap), wrap well and put in the fridge for 20 minutes.

Once the dough has chilled, roll out on a floured work surface to a neat rectangle 5 mm (¼ in) thick. Sprinkle the currants evenly on top of half of the rolled dough, and fold the uncovered half over the dried fruit to form a sandwich. Gently roll the giant garibaldi a little flatter using a rolling pin – some of the fruit will burst through the top layer of dough – and cut it into 4 x 7.5 cm (1½ x 3 in) fingers. Brush with milk, place on the prepared baking tray and bake for 12 minutes.

Peanut Butter Cookies

makes 15

–

*100 g (3½ oz) crunchy peanut butter • 75 g (2½ oz) butter, softened
125 g (4 oz/⅔ cup) soft brown sugar • 1 egg
150 g (5 oz/1¼ cups) plain (all-purpose) flour • ½ teaspoon salt
1 teaspoon baking powder*

A fabulous cakey peanut butter cookie, though you can substitute the nut of your choice using the nut butter recipe on page 104. This dough freezes beautifully: divide it into cookie-sized balls before freezing, then you can bake as many or as few as you like whenever you fancy.

method

Preheat the oven to 180°C (356°F/Gas 4) and line a baking tray with baking paper or a silicone mat.

Put the peanut butter, butter, sugar and egg in the cup of your blender and blitz to a smooth paste. Add the flour, salt and baking powder, stir and scrape down the sides to loosen the dough. Blitz, stir again and blitz one last time before wrapping in cling film (plastic wrap) and putting in the fridge for at least an hour and up to 24 hours.

Once the dough has chilled, roll into balls about the size of an apricot. Using the tines of a fork, flatten the balls onto the baking tray, leaving plenty of room between each cookie for spreading. Bake for 18 minutes.

Frozen

Making an easy ice cream that doesn't require churning or cooking complicated custards is a bit of a dream! These frozen treats just need a little forward planning, a small amount of room in your freezer and a spoon to enjoy. And if you want take your bullet blender to a whole new level then mixing cocktails in a blender is a lot of fun too and looks pretty impressive. Ideal for the summer months, or for recreating a holiday vibe at home.

Pistachio Ice Cream

makes 500 ml (17 oz/2 cups)

—

100 g (3½ oz/1¾ cups) nibbed or shelled unsalted pistachios
50 g (2 oz/¼ cup) caster (superfine) sugar • 20 g (¾ oz) Horlicks or Ovaltine powder
(or malted milk powder) • 250 g (9 oz) ready-to-eat custard (vanilla pudding)
50 ml (2 fl oz) double (heavy) cream • ½ teaspoon almond extract

Bright green, nutty pistachio ice cream was always my choice at ice cream parlours on holidays as a child. Who knew it was this easy to make at home.

method

Put the pistachios into the cup of your blender and blitz to a fine powder using the flat milling blade. Once almost all of the lumps have gone, add the sugar and Horlicks powder and blitz again. Making sure you've got all the sweet nut powder from the flat blade, switch to the four-pronged extraction blade, then add the remaining ingredients. Blitz to a smooth green paste. Pour into a freezer-proof dish and freeze for at least 4 hours.

Chocolate Coconut Parfait

serves 6
–

100 ml (3½ fl oz) double (heavy) cream
100 g (3½ oz) dark chocolate (minimum 70% cocoa), broken into pieces
250 ml (8½ fl oz) coconut cream · 100 g (3½ oz) Marshmallow Fluff spread

Coconut milk, marshmallow and ganache all freeze beautifully well, and enable this rich dessert to set into a silky smooth parfait without needing to churn or stir.

method

Bring the cream almost to the boil in a saucepan, or bowl if microwaving. Add the chocolate to the scalded cream and leave for 1 minute to melt, then stir into a smooth ganache and leave to cool. Put the cooled ganache into the cup of your blender first, then add the coconut cream and marshmallow spread and blitz until the ingredients have come together into a smooth, thick liquid. Pour into a freezer-proof dish or tub and freeze for about 2 hours.

Lemon Meringue Frozen Custard

makes 500 ml (17 oz/2 cups)

–

250 g (9 oz) lemon curd • 200 g (7 oz) ready-to-eat custard
juice of 1 lemon • 8 mini meringues, crushed
4 tablespoons Marshmallow Fluff spread

The sharp flavour of lemon with soft meringue and sticky mallow works a treat in this easy dessert.

method

Place the lemon curd, custard, lemon juice and half of the crushed meringues into the cup of your blender and blitz to mix well. Pour half of the lemon meringue custard into a freezer-proof container and dot half of the marshmallow spread around the surface of the custard, sprinkle on half of the remaining crushed meringues and cover with the rest of the lemon custard mix. Repeat the marshmallow spread and meringue process and run a spoon in a figure-of-eight pattern around the tub, to create a ripple. Close the lid and freeze for at least 4 hours.

Really Easy Chocolate Soft Serve

serves 4

–

3 small frozen bananas • 4 tablespoons Chocolate Spread (page 110)
a little milk (optional)

When I have overripe bananas in the fruit bowl, I peel and then freeze them in sandwich bags to use later in recipes like this.

method

Chop the frozen bananas into 1 cm (½ in) rounds and put into the cup of your blender with the chocolate spread. Blitz until smooth and fluffy; if it feels very thick, add a few tablespoons of milk. For the real ice-cream van experience, put into a piping bag with a large star nozzle attached and pipe out into an ice-cream cone.

Negroni Sorbet

serves 4

–

2 oranges, plus wedges to serve • 2 tablespoons bitter orange marmalade
3 tablespoons gin • 3 tablespoons red vermouth
90 ml (3 fl oz) Campari or Aperol • handful of ice

Not quite a cocktail, but more than a dessert,
this could be the ultimate sundowner.

method

Peel and segment the oranges, removing the pips,
and put in the freezer until frozen solid.

Once frozen, place the oranges in the cup of
your blender with the remaining ingredients and
blitz to a slush. Pour into a shallow tub and return
to the freezer for a further 2 hours. Serve in glasses
with a wedge of orange.

Frosé

serves 6

–

70 ml bottle of rosé (2¼ fl oz) • 200 g (7 oz) fresh strawberries
juice of ½ lemon • 1 teaspoon rose water
100 g (3½ oz/scant ½ cup) sugar • handful of ice cubes

Frozen rosé is a refreshing, fun cocktail for the summer months, and really easy to make too. It will keep for two weeks in the freezer; just reblitz to bring it back to life.

method

Empty the bottle of rosé into a wide plastic tray or tub and freeze for at least 5 hours.

Meanwhile, put the remaining ingredients, except the ice, into a saucepan, bring to the boil and gently simmer for 10 minutes, or until the strawberries have softened completely and given up most of their juice. Leave to cool.

Pass the strawberry and rose syrup through a sieve to remove the pips and put in the fridge until your rosé has frozen to a slush (it won't freeze completely solid because of the alcohol). Scrape the frozen rosé into the cup of your blender, along with the ice cubes and strawberry syrup. Blitz until smooth and serve in long glasses with a straw.

Watermelon Daiquiri

serves 2

–

½ small watermelon • 2 tablespoons simple sugar syrup (see opposite)
90 ml (3 fl oz) white rum • juice of 2 limes
handful of ice • 4 mint leaves

Simple sugar syrup is a useful thing to keep in the fridge, especially if you regularly make cocktails or sweet sauces. Weigh equal measures of sugar and water (it might feel odd to weigh water but this is the best way to do it) into a saucepan and simmer until the sugar has fully dissolved. Decanted into a sterilised bottle this will keep for up to four weeks in the fridge.

method

Cut and cube the watermelon flesh, and put in the freezer to set solid – this usually takes around 4 hours.

Add all the ingredients, with the exception of the mint leaves, to the cup of your blender and blitz until smooth. Once the ice and melon have been fully pulverised, add the mint leaves and give a final quick blitz. Pour into two long glasses and drink with a straw.

Land of Milk & Honey

serves 2
—

250 ml (8½ fl oz) mead (or Fuller's Honey Dew ale if you can't find mead)
100 ml (3½ fl oz) honey bourbon • 100 g (3½ oz) vanilla ice cream
1 tablespoon honey • handful of ice

This is the ultimate alcoshake – it tastes of honeyed ice cream with a grown-up edge.

method

Pour the mead or ale into a wide plastic tray or tub and freeze for at least 5 hours. Once the mead or ale has frozen, add it to the cup of your blender with the remaining ingredients and blitz to a thick, creamy shake.

Piña Colada Snow

serves 4

–

400 ml (14 fl oz) can coconut milk • 200 g (7 oz) pineapple, cut into chunks
75 ml (2½ fl oz) white rum • 15 g (½ oz) palm sugar
4 mint leaves

A refreshing, tropical slushie which is incredibly moreish – you can omit the rum and enjoy as a fun mocktail too.

method

Place the can of coconut milk in the fridge overnight. Taking care not to shake it, open carefully and spoon out the cream, which will have risen to the top. You can use this in cooking, or in the Chocolate Coconut Parfait on page 70.

You should be left with around 250 ml (8½ fl oz) of clear coconut milk. Pour this into an ice-cube tray and place in the freezer, along with the fresh pineapple.

After at least 4 hours, when the coconut milk and fruit have set solid, place them in the cup of your blender with the remaining ingredients. Blitz to a smooth slush and drink through a wide straw or eat with a spoon.

Bakewell Slush

serves 4
—

250 ml (8½ fl oz) brut Prosecco or cava
90 ml (3 fl oz) Chambord liqueur • 90 ml (3 fl oz) amaretto

A Christmassy cocktail which tastes like an almond and raspberry tart? Why ever not?!

method

Pour the sparkling wine into a wide plastic tray or tub and freeze for at least 5 hours. Once it has reached an even slush (it won't ever fully freeze because of its alcohol content) empty into the cup of your blender with the Chambord and amaretto and blitz to a fluffy slush. Pour into gin coupes or large wine glasses and enjoy.

Savoury Bites

Using your bullet blender to make herb and spice bases is the perfect springboard for mixing your own meatballs, pastry fillings and dumplings. These easy recipes can be adapted to make empanadas, pasties or ravioli once you get the hang of making mixes in your blender.

Sausage Rolls

makes 16

—

1 quantity of Rough Puff Pastry (page 52)
100 g (3½ oz) smoked streaky bacon, cut into 5 mm (¼ in) pieces
2 tablespoons thyme leaves • 2 tablespoons sage leaves
½ teaspoon ground nutmeg • ½ teaspoon salt • ½ teaspoon ground black pepper
zest of 1 lemon • 250 g (9 oz) minced (ground) pork
1 beaten egg for glazing • flaky sea salt to sprinkle

A homemade sausage roll, hot from the oven is a real treat.

method

Preheat the oven to 180°C (356°F/Gas 4) and line a baking tray with baking paper or a silicone sheet.

Put the bacon into the cup of your blender with all the seasonings, herbs and spices. Using the flat milling blade, blitz the bacon mix into a paste. Clear the bacon paste from the blades of the milling base and add the pork to the cup. Attach the four-pronged extraction blade and mix the pork with the herbed bacon paste.

On a well-floured surface, roll out the rough puff pastry to a 30 x 20 cm (12 x 8 in) rectangle and cut it in half lengthwise. Lay half of the bacon and pork mixture in a long, slim sausage, approximately 2.5 cm (1 in) thick along the 30 cm (12 in) edge of one of the pastry strips, leaving 1 cm (½ in) for a seam. Using a little beaten egg, wet the seam and bring the exposed pastry over the top of the sausage mix to create a sausage roll. Press the seam with a fork to seal it and slice the sausage roll into 2.5 cm (1 in) rounds and place on the baking tray. Repeat this process with the remaining pastry and sausage roll mix. Brush the sausage roll tops with the beaten egg and sprinkle with sea salt flakes before putting in the oven for 30 minutes, or until the pastry is risen and golden and the sausage meat has begun to brown.

Verde Mix

makes 200 g (7 oz/1 cup)

–

large bunch of mint • large bunch of parsley
1 small red onion, roughly chopped • zest of 1 lemon and juice of ½
½ teaspoon salt • ½ teaspoon ground black pepper
1 tomato, deseeded and chopped

This is a great herb base for meatballs, falafel and the delicious cracked wheat salad (pictured below), tabbouleh. You can play around with the quantities to suit your taste, or use it to make a fresh-tasting salad dressing by adding olive oil and red wine vinegar. However you use it, creating this fresh mix takes only minutes in your blender.

method

Remove the fresh herb leaves from their stalks and put in the cup of your blender. Add the remaining ingredients apart from the tomato and alternately blitz and shake the mixture in the cup until you have a chunky, chopped herb mix. Finally, stir in the chopped tomato and lemon juice.

Kofte

makes 12

–

250 g (9 oz) minced (ground) lamb • 40 g (1½ oz/¼ cup) pine nuts
100 g (3½ oz) Verde Mix (page 92) • 1 teaspoon ground cinnamon
1 teaspoon cumin seeds • ½ teaspoon chilli flakes

These lightly spiced, Middle Eastern kebabs
are so easy to prepare and show off the flavour
of the verde mix of herbs.

method

Place all the ingredients into the cup of your
blender and mix until you have a uniform meat
paste. Firmly squeeze the kofte mix into sausage
shapes, and grill (broil) or barbecue for
5–7 minutes each side.

Falafel

makes 12

–

150 g (5 oz) canned chickpeas, drained • 100 g (3½ oz) canned butter beans, drained
100 g (3½ oz) Verde Mix (page 92) • 3 garlic cloves
1 teaspoon ground coriander • 2 tablespoons sesame seeds
½ teaspoon cumin seeds • vegetable oil for deep-frying

Light, bright balls of flavour which make a lovely addition to a picnic.

method

Add the chickpeas and butter beans to the cup of your blender, and blitz with the milling blade until you have a smooth mixture. Add the remaining ingredients except the oil and blitz with the four-pronged extraction blade until you have a grainy paste. Using wet hands, form palm-sized balls and set aside in the fridge to chill for 30 minutes. Heat a large pan of oil, or a deep-fat fryer to 180°C (356°F/Gas 4), and fry the falafel in batches until golden brown. Drain on kitchen paper and eat while hot.

Pork & Prawn Pot Stickers

makes 25

–

250 g (9 oz) minced (ground) pork • 200 g (7 oz) raw peeled prawns (shrimps)
splash of soy sauce • 1 cm (½ in) chunk root ginger, peeled and roughly chopped
4 spring onions (scallions) • 1 garlic clove • pinch of sugar
½ teaspoon white pepper • 75 g (2½ oz) water chestnuts, sliced
4 chives • 25 dumpling skins (shop-bought or homemade)

Dim sum-style dumplings, which are fun to make and easy to prepare. You can pick up dumpling skins from the freezer section of health food shops and Asian supermarkets.

method

Put all the ingredients, except for the water chestnuts, chives and dumpling skins, into the cup of your blender and blitz in short bursts until you have a smooth paste. Add the water chestnuts and chives and blitz to a chunky mix.

Place a tablespoon of the mixture on one half of a dumpling skin. Using your finger, wet the edge and fold the skin over to create a semi-circular dumpling. Pinch the edges together and crimp. Pot stickers can be frozen to cook later or eaten immediately by frying in a hot, lightly oiled frying pan (skillet) for a few minutes until their bottoms are browned and crispy. Then, taking care the pan does not spit, pour in enough water to cover the bottom of the pan and cover with tin foil. Poke a few holes in the foil to enable the steam to escape and leave the dumplings to cook for 3–4 minutes until the water has evaporated. Carefully lift the dumplings out of the pan and enjoy dunked in soy sauce or a dipping sauce of your choice.

Veggie Pot Stickers

makes 25

–

*75 g (2½ oz) sliced water chestnuts • 150 g (5 oz) sweetheart or Japanese cabbage,
roughly chopped • 1 cm (½ in) chunk root ginger, peeled and roughly chopped
1 garlic clove, roughly chopped • 1 tablespoon sesame seeds • 6 chives
¼ teaspoon white pepper • 1 teaspoon rice wine vinegar • 1 tablespoon soy sauce
pinch of sugar • 50 g (2 oz) chestnut mushrooms, roughly chopped
25 dumpling skins (shop-bought or homemade)*

Crunchy water chestnut and sweet cabbage make it impossible to eat only one of these vegetarian dumplings!

method

Roughly chop half of the water chestnuts and place them in the cup of your blender with the cabbage, ginger and garlic. Using the flat milling blade, blitz to a grainy but even mixture. Add the sesame seeds, chives, pepper, vinegar, soy sauce and sugar and blitz to a paste. Lastly, chop the remaining water chestnuts and add with the mushrooms for one final blitz to mix.

Place a tablespoon of the mixture on one half of a dumpling skin. Using your finger, wet the edge and fold the skin over to create a semi-circular dumpling. Pinch the edges together and crimp. Pot stickers can be frozen to cook later or eaten immediately by frying in a hot, lightly oiled frying pan (skillet) for a few minutes until their bottoms are browned and crispy. Then, taking care the pan does not spit, pour in enough water to cover the bottom of the pan and cover with tin foil. Poke a few holes in the foil to enable the steam to escape and leave the dumplings to cook for 3–4 minutes until the water has evaporated. Carefully lift the dumplings out of the pan and enjoy dunked in soy sauce or a dipping sauce of your choice.

Spreads & Butters

Making your own spreads and pâtés is a very satisfying job. Many of these recipes can be packaged in nice jars and given as gifts – and no one need know how simple they were to make!

Toasted Almond Butter

makes 380 g (13½ oz/1½ cups)

–

*300 g (10½ oz/scant 2 cups) almonds • 80 ml (2¾ fl oz) almond oil
salt to taste*

Nut butters are so easy to make in your bullet blender. You can adapt this recipe to your favourite nut, or a combination of nuts.

method

Preheat the oven to 180°C (350°F/Gas 4). Spread the almonds evenly on a baking tray and toast in the oven for 15 minutes, then leave to cool.

Once cool enough to handle, put a handful into the cup of your blender. Using the flat milling blade, blitz in 5-second bursts, shaking the cup well between each blitz. Once all the nuts are milled to a fine powder, switch to the four-pronged extraction blade and add the almond oil and salt.

Blitz to a smooth butter. Tip into a sterilised container and enjoy on toast or as a dip.

Date & Cinnamon Caramel

makes 350g (12 oz/1½ cups)

–

200 g (7 oz) stoned dates • 150 ml (5 fl oz) boiling water
3 teaspoons ground cinnamon • 1 teaspoon ground ginger

Dates are so fantastically sweet that simply blitzing them with a few spices and some water will give you a delicious, refined sugar-free alternative to caramel, which is fabulous on toast, pancakes or even ice cream.

method

Soak the dates in the hot water. Add 2 teaspoons of the cinnamon, and ½ teaspoon of the ginger and leave to soak for 3–12 hours. Place everything, including the soaking water, in the cup of your blender and blitz until smooth. Put into a sterilised container and keep in the fridge for up to a week.

Biscuit Spread

makes 380 g (13½ oz/1½ cups)

–

100 g (3½ oz) Biscoff biscuits, broken into pieces
100 g (3½ oz/½ cup) soft brown sugar • 100 g (3½ oz) evaporated milk
4 teaspoons skimmed milk powder • 2 teaspoons salt • 1 teaspoon ground cinnamon
1 teaspoon ground ginger • 30 g (1 oz) butter, softened

Spiced brown sugar Speculoos spread, (or biscuit spread as it's known in my house), is becoming more widely available in supermarkets but it's so easy to make at home.

method
Put the biscuits into the cup of your blender with the sugar and blitz using the flat milling blade. Once you have a fine biscuit powder, add the remaining ingredients and blitz, using the four-pronged extraction blade, into a smooth spread. Tip into a sterilised jar and keep in the fridge for up to 4 weeks. Enjoy on toast, ice cream or as a dip for fruit.

Chocolate Spread

makes 700 g (24½ oz/3 cups)

–

100 g (3½ oz/⅔ cup) blanched hazelnuts • 300 g (10½ oz) evaporated milk
200 g (7 oz) milk chocolate, broken into pieces (or milk chocolate chips)
50 g (2 oz/¼ cup) caster (superfine) sugar • 50 g (2 oz) skimmed milk powder
½ teaspoon vanilla extract • ½ teaspoon flaky sea salt

A super-easy chocolate-nutty spread that's great on toast and pancakes, as well as in recipes such as the **Chocolate Melt-in-the-middle Puddings** on page 26.

method

Preheat the oven to 180°C (356°F/Gas 4). Spread the hazelnuts evenly on a baking tray and toast for 10 minutes. Once cooled, put the nuts in the cup of your blender and blitz to a fine powder using the flat milling blade.

Meanwhile, bring the evaporated milk to almost boiling point in a saucepan or microwave, add the chocolate and leave for about 2 minutes until it has melted, then stir to a smooth paste. Place the chocolate mixture, sugar, milk powder and vanilla into the cup of your blender with the powdered hazelnuts and blend to a smooth paste with the four-pronged extraction blade. Add the salt, give a final blitz and pour into a sterilised jar. Leave to cool, then keep in the fridge for up to 2 weeks, to enjoy on toast or use in other recipes.

Chicken Liver Pâté

makes 500 g (17½ oz/2 cups)

–

150 g (5 oz) butter, softened, plus a knob for the bacon
3 rashers thin-cut smoked streaky bacon, cut into 5 mm (¼ in) strips
1 banana shallot (eschalion), chopped • 1 garlic clove, chopped
1 teaspoon thyme leaves • 200 g (7 oz) chicken livers, trimmed and cleaned
3 tablespoons bourbon whisky • ¼ teaspoon ground nutmeg
¼ teaspoon salt • ¼ teaspoon ground black pepper

This pâté is rich and luxurious and a real treat on toast – the kind of thing that elevates a lunch and is so simple to make.

method

Place 50 g (2 oz) of the butter in a heatproof bowl and gently melt in a moderate oven or microwave until completely liquid. Leave to separate into clarified butter and whey. Discard the milky whey and retain the clarified butter for sealing the pâté.

Meanwhile, put the bacon into a medium saucepan with a knob of butter to help the bacon fat to melt. Add the shallot, garlic and thyme leaves and sauté for 10 minutes until the bacon is cooked through, though not in any way crispy, and the shallot is translucent. Put the chicken livers into the pan and fry for a few minutes each side. Don't overcook them, or they will become gritty. Add the bourbon and simmer for a minute, then transfer the contents of the pan to the cup of your blender. Add the nutmeg, salt, pepper and 50 g (2 oz) of the butter, and blitz to a smooth pâté. Stir and scrape down the sides before adding the remaining butter and blitzing again.

Smooth the pâté into ramekins or a small serving dish and pour the clarified butter over the top to create an airtight seal. Chill in the fridge for at least an hour before serving.

Smoked Mackerel Pâté

makes 400 g (14 oz/1½ cups)

–

2 smoked mackerel fillets, flaked • 150 g (5 oz) cream cheese
50 g (2 oz) crème fraîche • 1 tablespoon horseradish sauce • 1 tablespoon fresh dill
½ teaspoon ground black pepper • squeeze of lemon juice

A firm favourite for a light dinner, and one that is a cinch to make at home.

method

Add half of the mackerel to the cup of your blender along with the cream cheese, crème fraîche, horseradish, dill and pepper. Blitz to a smooth paste – you might need to scrape down the sides and stir a few times to ensure a good mix. Add the remaining flaked mackerel and stir through the pâté together with the squeeze of lemon. Spoon into a sterilised jar; the pâté will keep up to 3 days in the fridge.

Chestnut & Red Wine Pâté

makes 400 g (14 oz/1½ cups)

–

*65 g (2¼ oz) butter • 2 banana shallots (eschalions), chopped
50 g (2 oz) mushrooms, chopped • 150 ml (5 fl oz) red wine
4 sprigs of thyme • 1 bay leaf • salt and ground black pepper to taste
250 g (9 oz) chestnut purée*

A hearty vegetarian pâté which is also wonderful wrapped in rough puff pastry, baked and served 'en croute'.

method

Heat 15 g (½ oz) of the butter in a saucepan and gently sauté the shallots. After 5 minutes add the mushrooms and continue to cook until tender.

Pour in the red wine, add the herbs and simmer, reducing the wine by half and adding the remaining butter. Season to taste, remove the thyme sprigs and bay leaf and transfer the mixture to the cup of your blender along with the chestnut purée. Blitz to a smooth pâté and spoon into a sterilised jar or ramekin. Chill in the fridge for at least an hour.

Dips
& Sauces

Whether you're batch-cooking to fill your freezer or hosting a barbecue, these dips and sauces are scrumptious, simple to make and easily adaptable to your own taste.

Guacamole

makes 350g (12 oz/1½ cups)

—

small bunch of coriander (cilantro)
4 spring onions (scallions), white and green parts separated • ½ teaspoon salt
flesh of 1 lime • 1 small red chilli • 1 tomato, deseeded and roughly chopped
2 ripe avocados, flesh scooped out and roughly chopped

Adding the flesh of the lime not only gives this guacamole a fresh burst of flavour but also maintains the dip's vibrant green colour for longer.

method

Remove and discard the lower stalks of the coriander, leaving mostly leaves. Place the coriander in the cup of your blender with the whites of the spring onions, salt, lime flesh and chilli (use less chilli if you're not keen on the heat).

Blitz to a chunky pulp. Roughly chop the green stalks of the spring onions and add to the cup with the tomato and avocados. Blitz to bring together into a chunky guacamole. Add more salt, lime or chilli according to taste.

White Bean Hummus

makes 350g (12 oz/1½ cups)
—

400 g (14 oz) can butter beans (lima beans) • 1 small garlic clove
2 tablespoons peanut or almond butter • juice of 1 lemon
pinch of salt • 4 tablespoons olive oil

Using canned butter beans makes life very simple, especially if you are pressed for time, but if you decide to cook the beans from dry, remember to reserve some of the cooking water.

method

Drain the beans, reserving the water they have been packaged in. Put 100 ml (3½ fl oz) of the bean water and all the other ingredients into the cup of your blender and blitz to a smooth purée, shaking the cup occasionally to make sure all the beans have been pulverised. If the hummus feels too thick, add a little more of the reserved bean water.

Beetroot Hummus

makes 350g (12 oz/1½ cups)
–

200 g (7 oz) canned chickpeas, drained and water reserved
1 medium beetroot (beet), cooked and peeled • 2 teaspoons horseradish sauce
2 tablespoons olive oil • 1 teaspoon chopped fresh dill
juice of ½ lemon • salt to taste

A delicious dip, and one that goes brilliantly with the Kofte or Falafel on pages 94 and 96. If you decide to cook the chickpeas from dry, be sure to reserve some of the cooking water.

method

Put 2 tablespoons of the reserved chickpea water and the rest of the ingredients, except the salt, into the cup of your blender and blitz to a smooth, pink purée. Add salt to taste, and store in the fridge for up to 3 days.

Pea Purée

makes 400 g (14 oz/1½ cups)
–

200 g (7 oz) cauliflower, broken into florets • 150 g (5 oz) frozen peas
2 tablespoons milk • 20 g (¾ oz) softened butter • a few mint leaves
salt and ground black pepper to taste

This came about as a result of a craving for mushy peas, but is so much more refined than its inspiration. It is delicious served hot with fish and chips, or chilled on bruschetta with a shaving of Parmesan.

method

Boil or steam the cauliflower for 10 minutes until just tender, and defrost the peas by sitting them in boiling water for 5 minutes. Drain both vegetables and leave for 10 minutes to cool.

Put the cauliflower, milk, butter, mint and 100 g (3½ oz) of the peas into the cup of your blender and blitz to a smooth, creamy purée. Crush the remaining peas with the back of a fork and add to the purée, stir and season to taste.

Aïoli

makes 150 g (5 oz/½ cup)
–

2 egg yolks • juice of ½ lemon • ½ teaspoon mustard powder
1 small garlic clove • ½ teaspoon salt • 160 ml (5½ fl oz) olive oil
ground black pepper to taste

A very easy garlic mayonnaise, which is fantastic on boiled eggs or used as a dip for crudités or chips (fries).

method

Put all the ingredients, except the olive oil, into the cup of your blender. Add 40 ml (1½ fl oz) of the olive oil and blitz, using the flat milling blade, for three 10-second bursts. Add a further 40 ml (1½ fl oz) of oil and repeat the blitzing pattern. Do this until you have used all of the oil and have a thick mayonnaise. Add more salt and pepper to your taste and decant into a sterilised jar; the aïoli will keep for 1 week in the fridge.

Please note: this recipe uses uncooked egg, so is not advisable for consumption by pregnant women or those with compromised immune systems.

Salsa Verde

makes 250 g (9 oz/1 cup)
–

small bunch of mint • large bunch of flat-leaf parsley • small bunch of basil
small bunch of tarragon • 6 anchovies • 1 tablespoon capers
1 tablespoon Dijon mustard • 1 tablespoon red wine vinegar • juice of ½ lemon
2 garlic cloves • 120 ml (4 fl oz) extra virgin olive oil

This is a classic sauce for serving with fish, meat or roast vegetables. It's very quick and simple to make in your blender, and using this basic recipe you can mix and match the herbs to suit your taste. Leave out the anchovies if you don't eat fish, but be sure to add plenty of salt if you do.

mustard, vinegar, lemon juice and garlic and, using the flat milling blade, blitz to a green paste. Add the olive oil a tablespoon at a time, blitzing between each addition until you have a thick, green paste of spoonable consistency (you may not need to use all of the oil). The salsa verde will keep for a day in the fridge.

method

Strip all the herbs from their stems, and put in the cup of your blender. Add the anchovies, capers,

Chunky Pesto

makes 150 g (5 oz/½ cup)

–

75 ml (2½ fl oz) olive oil • 50 g (2 oz/⅓ cup) pine nuts
3 tablespoons basil leaves, roughly chopped
30 g (1 oz) Parmesan or Grana Padano, grated • ½ garlic clove

Pesto is a delicious, quick and easy way to dress pasta, salads or soups. Once you've got the hang of the quantities, you'll find making pesto with your favourite combination of herbs and nuts is so simple that you'll never want to eat shop-bought pesto again! This makes enough for six large servings on pasta; I tend to make this amount and freeze it in ice-cube trays to use whenever I'm in a hurry.

method

Reserving half of the olive oil, put all the ingredients into the cup of your blender. Blitz until the leaves have been fully pulverised and there are still chunks of pine nut visible. Add half of the reserved olive oil, shake or stir the pesto and blitz again. Then stir in the remaining oil to finish the pesto, giving it a pourable consistency. Serve immediately or freeze for later.

Goat's Cheese
& Walnut Pesto

makes 150 g (5 oz/½ cup)

–

50 g (2 oz/scant ½ cup) walnuts • 3 tablespoons basil leaves
100 g (3½ oz) soft goat's cheese • 2 tablespoons olive oil
¼ teaspoon ground black pepper

This tangy goat's cheese sauce is ideal for stirring into pasta or spreading on toast.

method

Place the walnuts and basil into the cup of your blender and blitz using the flat milling blade.

Dislodge any mixture stuck beneath the blade and add the goat's cheese, oil and pepper, then blitz again into a chunky, spreadable sauce. The pesto will keep in the fridge for 3 days.

Creamy Butternut Squash Pasta Sauce

makes 400 g (14 oz/1½ cups)
–

300 g (10½ oz) butternut squash, peeled and cubed • 3 garlic cloves
1 red onion, roughly chopped • 4 sprigs of thyme • 8 tablespoons olive oil
4 tablespoons water • salt and ground black pepper to taste

Despite containing no dairy, this hearty, smooth sauce is naturally creamy thanks to the butternut squash. It is delicious on filled pasta like ravioli, or on thick ribbon pasta with more fresh thyme sprinkled on top.

method

Preheat the oven to 170°C (325°F/Gas 3). Spread the squash, garlic, onion and thyme on a baking tray. Drizzle over half of the olive oil and roast for 35–40 minutes, turning occasionally until the onion and squash have completely softened. Once the vegetables have cooled, remove the thyme sprigs and put the roasted veggies and remaining oil into the cup of your blender and blitz. Add the water and blitz again until you have a smooth, creamy sauce. Season to taste with salt and black pepper.

This sauce can be kept in the fridge for up to 3 days or frozen in portion-sized sandwich bags to use whenever you need.

About the Author

Juliet Baptiste-Kelly

–

Juliet Baptiste-Kelly trained in fine art, and spent ten years working in marketing before finally acknowledging the fact that she was far more interested in catering the events she was organising than running them. She retrained as a baker and pastry chef before becoming a food stylist and home economist for print, film and television. She lives in south-east London with her husband and two children.

Acknowledgements

Thanks to Kate Pollard, Ruby Bender, Jacqui Melville (and Radar the Studio Dog) for bringing my recipe scribblings and random notes to life, making everything look so gorgeous, while also putting the world to rights. Also to Claire Warner for the fabulous layout design and everyone at Hardie Grant for being so enthusiastic and kind.

Thank you too to Catherine Arnold for whizzing up a brownie in her blender and sparking the idea for this book.

Huge thanks to my indefatigable parents, Glena and Eric, to Jodi Bradford and to Paula Flack, who so regularly pick up the slack (and the children) on my rather peripatetic job. Massive thanks to my work wife and small, ginger champion Vic Grier.

And lastly, deepest thanks and boundless love to John, Art and Agnes for being patient, understanding, eager recipe testers and the most awesome family a girl could hope for.

Index

Blitz by Juliet Baptiste-Kelly

ISBN: 978-1-78488-136-8

First published in 2018
by Hardie Grant Books,
an imprint of Hardie
Grant Publishing

Hardie Grant Books (UK)
52–54 Southwark Street
London SE1 1UN

Hardie Grant Books (Australia)
Ground Floor, Building 1
658 Church Street
Melbourne, VIC 3121

hardiegrantbooks.com

Publisher: Kate Pollard
Senior Editor: Kajal Mistry
Desk Editor: Molly Ahuja
Publishing Assistant: Eila Purvis
Design: Claire Warner Studio
Photography: © Jacqui Melville
Prop Styling: Tonia Shuttleworth
and Ginger Whisk
Styling Assistant: Ruby Bender
Author portrait on page 138:
© Anna Batchelor
Copy editor: Lorraine Jerram
Proofreader: Kay Halsey
Indexer: Cathy Heath
Colour Reproduction by p2d
Printed and bound at Toppan
Leefung, DongGuan City, China